# How to Deal with Stress and Live a Harmonic Life
## 15 easy steps

# Your Gift

I wanted to show my appreciation that you support my work so I've put together a free gift for you.

http://bonusfreebook.org/

Just visit the link above to download it now.

I know you will love this gift.

If you like this book, you can see and buy my other books on this link:

*ALL BOOKS OLIVER SMITH HERE*

*Thank you for attention!*

*With love,*

*OLIVER SMITH*

Contents



**Introduction**

Many are times that we get into situations that leave us unwell mentally and even sometimes in the long run physically. This book is out to seek a better understanding of stress, its causes, and solutions. I am also going to look into various ways of making sure that one does not fall into stress. Stress is mostly related to someone having so multiple demanding situations that the brain gets overwhelmed. In the current times, life is full of many dynamics. We get to deal with a ton of things like work, family, bills, school and many others.

Today, everything in our life requires perfection to achieve success and this makes many people struggling to reach it to give up trying. Evidently that we are faced with situations that may leave us in stress, the difference comes in where we ought to bounce back. Some people let themselves be under stress and that ends up adversely messing up their lives. Others are able to look for help and pull themselves out of the stress pit. There are also those who have found the secret of a healthy state of the mind, and never even find themselves getting stressed out from time to time.

In this book, I seek to bring out the difference among these three types of people. What does one need to make sure they avoid stress? What do you have to do when you find yourself in stressful situations? What are the secrets for healthy living? I intend to answer these questions in this book.

Stress has become a common thing in today's modern society and I feel enough has not been said and done. Awareness has to be created to ensure we manage stress in the society. Anyone can be a victim of stress, and that is the main reason I wrote this book. So I would like to help people facing a stressful situation and give some recommendations to deal with stress.

**Chapter 1**

## What is stress?

Many times, we fail to understand the true meaning of stress. What do people exactly mean saying that they are stressed? Stress can be explained as an emotional or mental tension that is caused by circumstances around the person. Mostly stress comes from demanding circumstances either at home or at the workplace. It can basically come from anything that we are exposed to. However, some people are more vulnerable to stress than others. This is mostly as a result of our different personalities. Stress can be termed as a physical response to some emotional pressure. During stress periods, the body feels and reacts drastically by producing a mix of hormones like adrenaline in preparation for physical reactions like fight or flight. However, stress sometimes can be the main reason for low self-esteem. And all too often, it causes depression that can be explained as prolonged stress.

Surprisingly, it has been proved that gender is also a determinant of our vulnerability to stress. The World Health Organization asserts that a large number of women depressed all over the world as compared to men. However, different researchers have shown that the male gender is more vulnerable to stress than the female gender. A man is more likely to be worn down by stress than a woman when facing the same situation. The difference mostly comes in our biological composition. Women are created to persevere through sometimes harsh conditions than men. This makes men a bit inferior since we break into stress immediately we are faced with a problem. Women are said to be more likely to get social stress.

This is stress caused by social relationships for instance loss of loved ones, breakups and divorce and even friendship scuffles. On the other hand, men are most likely to be stressed because of work problems, family issues and many other stressful events around them.

In addition, women are able to fight stress better than men because they easily open up and talk about their feelings to friends and family. Naturally, men are unable to speak out and express their feelings. The society expects a man to be tough all the time. It is termed as a weakness for a man to open up and express his feelings.

Over the years, stress has been termed by many as the 'silent killer'. This is a term that was deduced from the lethal health implications stress has. Stress can lead to high blood pressure, heart diseases, cancer, stroke, chest pains and in some cases an irregular heartbeat.

There has been a myth that has been around for centuries that stress turns your hair grey. It is actually not a myth or a misconception, rather it is a fact and it is scientifically proven. Moreover, stress is a reason for hair loss. It, however, comes even after stressful situations are over. Specialists encourage people to be constantly laughing and try to be happy since laughter releases hormones that lower stress levels in a person. The more some people laugh the more they are producing hormones that counter stress.

According to CNN, the main reason of stress in the world currently is money.         The countries least stressed about finances are Russia, Italy, and France. The U.S.A, China, Singapore, and Malaysia are world`s most stressed countries.

Everyone is getting themselves worked up over money and wealth. Finally, stress should not be termed as completely evil. If it were not for the early man being stressed due to hardship, there would have been no innovations and inventions to make worse easier. Stress from day to day life caused by humans to learn how to survive and think of ways of improving living conditions.

## Causes of stress

Stress can be categorized into two groups according to the time: long-term stress and short-term stress. Short-term stress is a stressful situation that comes from one-time things like taking a test, running races, going on a date and many other minor things. Long-term stress, on the other hand, is such type of stress caused by long-term situations. These are problems that are recurring and happen often. Mostly long-term stress can be the result of work hardships, marriage or health reasons. Long-term stress also known as a chronic stress is extremely dangerous since it results in body weakness giving way to adverse health implications. Stress can be caused by both personal and social-economic issues. Personal issues include:

1. Loss of a loved one. Some major life changes like the death of a loved one often the reason to be stressed. This is mostly due to the life changes people have to make after losing a loved one. For example, some routine changes and this may lead to some type of stress.

2. Divorce or other marital issues. Getting married on its own is a cause of stress due to the change in lifestyle that the couple undergoes. Divorce now even makes its worse. Married people are mostly very close. Almost the best friends. When divorce happens, it affects the

couple strongly and causes emotional hurt and sometimes even social pressures.

3.  Loss of employment. Life during this current time is full of bills here and there. Nothing comes free in the world anymore. We have to pay for electricity, rent, water, and many other obligations that come with survival. Employment keeps people going and a sense of monetary security since there is an expected paycheck at some point. When a person loses employment they mostly lose their source of livelihood so stress comes from seeing that you cannot provide for your family anymore due to your lack of employment. In the United States, unemployment has been a major problem causing stress and even suicide in some situations.

4.  An increase in the financial budget obligations. Stress is mostly as a result of        a change in routine. When someone was not used to cater for some financial obligations, and for one reason or another he/she starts catering to them, stress may come. A good example is a new couple having a baby. The first few months are hell since both parents were not used to the new financial obligation. An extra mouth to feed and all other obligations that come with a baby.

5. Moving to a new home. Moving to a new city is never an easy thing. It mostly means leaving an entire life behind. Friends, places you love, customs you used to and even letting go of some precious memories. When someone moves to a new place, they feel a bit empty for a while since they don't have friends or even people they know very well and trust. This emptiness feeling leads to stress. Mostly this type of stress is called as 'homesickness'.

6. Injury or chronic illness to oneself or people around. Health issues like terminal diseases cause severe stress. Being a caregiver to a person in pain also puts you in a stressful situation because they experience pain and it hurts you internally. According to studies, in most couples where one takes care of the other due to illness or injury, the caregiver ends under intensive stress. Some patients, mostly cancer patients, end up dying sooner than they should have as a result of stress. They are depressed and start believing that the situation cannot be fought. This stress makes them weaker and leads to  earlier death than expected.

7. Heavy workload upon one's self. This is one of the major reasons of stress among men. With bills and the pressure of being rich, people tend to work extra hard. Nowadays, it is not a new thing seeing

people alternating even four jobs in one day. The pressure of living an expensive lifetime makes people work more than their bodies can handle. This excessive strain on the body affects even the mind leading to stress. The stress is because the body and mind are undergoing strain trying to keep up with things they are naturally able to handle.

8. Dangerous conditions at the workplace. Some jobs are dangerous for our life. For example, some jobs like being a soldier or working in chemical industries.  However, they have to be done so that we can earn a living. People working in these sectors know how much they are risking and this causes stress in their lives. For soldiers mostly in the war, you can never be sure of coming back home. Every day you wake up you stay in a constant state of fear not knowing what will happen tomorrow. This fear and anxiety lead to stress.

9. Discrimination from colleagues. Bullying has been an issue that has existed for many centuries. However, things have gotten worse lately with the various technology inventions in communication that has resulted in many social internet platforms. The platforms were initially created to impact on the society positively. On the contrary, these platforms have become a new method of bullying. Cyberbullying has

been the reason of stress for many people. People air their opinions about others online not caring about the emotional hurt it causes. This is mostly a trend among young people. They write hurtful things on social networks about their colleagues. Some people even commit suicide as a result of this bullying related stress since they feel too ashamed to live anymore.

**10.**     Post-traumatic stress. The brain is usually like a camcorder. What we see through our eyes is recorded and stored by the brain. When someone undergoes a traumatic experience, it sometimes affects them mentally causing stress. People who have undergone experiences like rape, war or even serious accidents end up getting some kind of fear that causes some stress. They are unable to forget the things they witnessed. This stress caused by traumatic experiences is referred to as post-traumatic stress disorder or acute stress disorder. It is very common among soldiers or people that have experienced war or other light threatening experiences.

## Stresses and our routine

Stress is quite hazardous in our daily lives. It has adverse effects on our wellbeing both physical and emotional. Stress can cause certain illness or even death in extreme situations. Stress causes the wear and tear of many internal organs like the heart. This can lead to death or serious heart disorders.

Stress also causes the gradual depreciation of immune system leaving a person to be more vulnerable to many illnesses. It can also affect our relationships with loved ones since dealing with a stressed human being is a hard task and many people are unable to cope with it. In addition, stress seriously affects our work performance and general productivity of a person.

In relation to stress, a routine is a positive reliever of stress. Routine reduces stress because the body automatically does some daily activities. Women realized that some routines help them to reduce their stresses as mothers and wives due to the daily tasks they are faced with.

On the other hand, changes in routine also may be as some reasons of stress. Humans are happy staying in an environment where they do the same things day in day out. The routine gives a person a good sense of laxity in a comfort zone. Once this is over, and things have to change, someone might develop stress. The main reason is moving to a new home or even divorce and loss of loved ones. All these cause stress is the change in routine that someone was used to.  When people divorce, they have to change their lifestyle from married back to single. This two are seriously different lifestyles.

## Why are you stressed out?

In our day to day lives, we are forced to deal with very many tasks. We have family, jobs and many other responsibilities like tax and bills. Human brains were not designed to process all that information in a go. Due to this incorporation of all these functions in one brain, we end up getting stressed. It is, therefore, true to say that stress is a result of overworking our brains trying to handle everything at the same time. Life also sometimes gives us a lot of 'lemons'. We are faced with some dramatizing situations that we are unable to get off the mind: violence, wars, rape, accidents and many others. Witnessing this incidence leaves very many people messed up mentally. Generally, many people are stressed due to the high demands put upon us by life.

## Negative thoughts

According to Russ Harris in the book *'The Happiness Trap',* 80% of thoughts of everyone contain some sort of negativity. It is quite normal to have thoughts that are negative. People have a default thought system that constantly scans for negativity in everything. Having negative thoughts is normal as a human being, however, when you start believing in those thoughts is when things start going south and stress starts to encroach on. When we start believing in these negative thoughts we get fused with the false stories and we fail to see other better perspectives in situations, places, and people around us. The only trick towards pushing away negative thinking is keeping your mind in check of what you're thinking. Try to twist and modify every negative thought to either positive or neutral perspective.

# Chapter 2

**How to reduce stress**

Stress is a serious 'disease' that can lead to an extreme fatal ending. We need to make away with stress to live happy lives and interact better with our loved ones. This chapter about the various ways of removing stress. These ways are well researched by expert psychological specialists all around the world. Many people have their various opinions of eradicating stress. We always try to find the perfect solution for stress, some people may think drugs like alcohol and even conventional medication can remove stress. That is usually a very misguided ideology. They only make you forget the problems at that time when you are using them. Afterward, when you get back to the right state of mind, you remember the stresses and it all comes back again. The best way is to identify the reason for the stress and then deal with it in its own special way. Below are some effective ways of removing stress:

## 1. Switch off your anxiety

Sanne van Rooij, Ph.D., and Anais Stenson, PhD., explain anxiety as a disorder that causes a person to be worried and fearful at all times. Anxiety can be described as a disorder that progresses over time and keeps getting more and more severe. Anxiety is a normal emotion. However, when it progresses and becomes more frequent than normal it causes stress. Anxiety can be caused by past events or fear of the unknown. Getting rid of anxiety is one of the most important ways of relieving stress. Anxiety can be switched off by finding inner calmness, relaxation, and serenity. This can be done through many ways. ☐

Meditation: through meditation, you are able to switch of all external forces and deeply concentrate on yourself. In meditation, you should focus on things that make you happy and avoid sad thoughts. It is also advised that meditation is much more effective than medication.

Deep breathing: anxiety comes from within and calming the 'inner person' both emotionally and physically is a way of eradicating anxiety. Through deep breathing, one calms down and relaxes. By concentrating on the breathing one is able to forget everything.

Practicing self-care: once you take care of yourself, the body gets a feeling of being more rewarded and hence more comfortable and relaxed. Self-care is through various activities like body massages, dressing better, eating healthy and even associating with positively minded folks. ☐

Through the above-mentioned practices, one can easily remove anxiety and in the long run, stress is relieved. There are many more ways of rewarding the body. It is hard to tackle all of them since different people have different personalities and therefore diversity of interests. It's therefore advised that anytime anxiety kicks in, you find your own way of calming yourself.

## 2. Understand your emotions.

Emotions are sensory perceptions that affect our behavior and relation with the people around us. Our emotions greatly affect our perception of things, either positive or negative. In return, these perceptions dictate how we react to things and situations. Negative emotions lead to stress or even at extreme time depression. In order to remove stress, we need to understand our emotions and know how to deal with them. For instance, many people do not know how to react to anger. The wrong reaction to this emotion can cause a person to fall into deep stress. Another example is sadness. When someone is sad and they fail to know how to deal with it, stress starts encroaching and the sadness even worsens resulting in worse fatalities.

### 3. Change your thoughts.

Famous actor and martial artist Bruce Lee said that '*the greatest weapon against stress is our ability to choose one thought over another*'. Our thoughts greatly dictate how we feel. Negative thoughts mostly lead to people being stressed. We need to take charge of our thoughts and make sure we leave no room for negative thoughts in order to eradicate stress. Any time a negative thought comes, it is advised to twist it and train your brain to see the positivity of things.

### 4. Express your stress creatively.

Positivity is the key ingredient is relieving stress. Everyone has stress in one way or another. It might be family, work, school or even relationships with friends. The way we perceive the stress determines whether we will get stressed or not. When we are faced with a situation, one should view it positively. Obstacles or problems once viewed as learning tools become easier to deal with. Every situation teaches as a way to learn new things and get stronger. '*What doesn't kill you makes you stronger*'.

### 5. Believe in your success

Famous pastor and evangelist Joel Osteen once said that '*I believe that God has put gifts and taints and ability on the inside of every one of us. When you develop that and you believe that you're a person of influence and a person of purpose, I believe you can rise up out of any situation'.* The first step towards getting out of stress is believing that you are able and not letting anyone or anything convince you otherwise. A positive state of mind allows a person to pull out of anything. When you believe that you are able to pull out of stress and solve whatever is stressing you out, you gain power over it. You gain a command of your mind and body and pulling out becomes even easier than expected. Self-confidence is a vital ingredient in eradicating stress out of a person.

# Chapter 3

**Harmonious life**

Sanskrit religious text from the second millennium BC states that *'yesterday is only a dream and tomorrow is only a vision; but today, well lived, makes every yesterday a dream of happiness and every tomorrow a vision of hope'*. What is a harmonious life? Harmony is usually described as a rhythmic synchronization of various entities to produce good results. Harmony is associated with the success of many things including teams and other activities involving different entities working together. Consequently, a harmonious life is a life where various entities of one's self-are well taken care of and in return, they work together for the well being of the entire body. For our body to be termed as healthy, all the working parts need to be well functioning and maintained. A harmonious life is a life where the body, mind, and soul are well fed and taken care of to a level of total satisfaction. This achievement of comfort helps to reduce strain on the body and mind that causes stress. Below are various ways of achieving a harmonious life:

- Eat healthy food.

A healthy body is a healthy state of mind. Healthy food nourishes the body and allows a person to be more productive. Healthy eating is one of the best ways to reward the body and even chase away health stresses like illnesses and fatigue. It is therefore advised that one should eat healthy so as to maintain a nourished body that is free from illnesses. Many people that have had long and comfortable lives all attest that one of the secrets of a long healthy life is the food we consume. The body processes and in return produces what we ingest. If you live on an unhealthy diet, the body will be unhealthy and even develop some ailments like the rapidly growing problem of obesity.

- Exercises for your body

American former president John F. Kennedy once said that *'physical fitness is not only one of the most important keys to a healthy body, it is the basis of dynamic and creative intellectual activity'*. When the body is healthy, we are even in a better position to be more productive even mentally. This is the harmony I was talking about earlier. When the body and mind are well taken care of, we get more productive in all aspects and even avoid stress better. We get stronger and healthier in all aspects of our being. Exercise allows a person to have increased inner awareness and general body harmony. Exercise transforms human consciousness with the body giving the body and minds the nourishment needed to block out stress and other negative forces. Nowadays, there are many forms of exercises and this diversity in choices even makes it easier for people to exercise and be healthy. Currently, most common ways are yoga and Zumba. Yoga is a deep meditation incorporated with muscle stretching and body relaxation. Yoga allows a person to be in touch with the inner self at the same time building the physical body. It's a great and innovative way of exercising body and mind without vigorous exercise.

- Exercise for your mind

Brain exercises are a great way of relaxing our mind. Mind exercises can be done through various ways. These ways include: listening to soothing music of one's taste, testing recall ability by trying to remember things that happened in the past, taking foreign languages courses and cooking or baking, challenging one's taste buds, taking part in mind games like chess and drawing mental maps of places to see mental ability. There are many more ways of exercising the mind:

- Relaxation

Relaxing the body highly relieves stress. A settled body is a settled mind. Through taking massages and vacations allows the body to relax and relieve day to day stresses. People need some time to go away from daily routine and focus on themselves to relax. It is quite healthy for one to take some time off from work or school and relax. This greatly helps in resting and removing the stressful situations that come with day-to-day life.

Mostly, relaxation comes from participating in leisure activities and hobbies that we like. These activities help us to expel the negative energy we build up in daily hustles. It is important to find something that you like and then make it a habit every once in a while. This activity greatly assists in achieving mental and body relaxation from the struggles we undergo in our lives.

- Spiritual life

Getting in touch with one's spiritual life allows us to quench the thirst for the soul. Spiritual nourishment gives the heart a special type of contentment and feeling of fulfillment. Being in touch with spiritual life gives the heart a special relaxation and helps in remaining positive to keep away stress. Through praying we are able to let go and move on. Through praying, people can share stresses and problems with a supernatural power. The faith acquired in spiritual life is a great part of a harmonious living.

## Conclusion

Every day of our lives we are faced with various obstacles lead to some stress. However, how we perceive the stress determines if we fall into depression or we pull out of the stress. Positivity is the most important thing in ensuring that we are not put down by stress. Allowing ourselves to fall into stress can result in fatalities including death or illness. It is important that we follow the guide towards keeping away stress through positive emotions and perceptions of things happening in our lives. We should completely ensure that we do not give way to stress. In the occasion that we under the stress, it is also important that we immediately seek help and start the recovery process as soon as possible to avoid falling into depression which is a disease. We need to connect more with our inner self and relax our bodies and mind. Taking care of our physical body is a great way towards living healthy and keeping away stress. ☐